Kidpower™ Safety Comics

An Introduction to "People Safety" for
Young Children Ages 3 to 10 and Their Adults

Irene van der Zande
Illustrated by Amanda Golert

A Publication of Kidpower Teenpower Fullpower International
Committed to creating a safer world for everyone, everywhere

Acknowledgements

Thank you to our Cartoon Power Team:

The contributions of many people have made these materials possible. The creative concepts, writing, and production leadership are the work of Kidpower Co-Founder, Executive Director and Author, Irene van der Zande. The cover and cartoons are drawn by Kidpower Curriculum and Training Consultant and Swedish Center Director, Amanda Golert. Allegra Doriss, Chantal Keeney, Erika Leonard, Beth McGreevy, and April Yee have each provided important help with layout, design, editing, and production. Translation into Spanish was done by Silvia Austerlic, Cassie Canfield, and Gema Lopez-Smith. Ed van der Zande donated time to find funding.

Thank you to Ian Price of Price Watkins Media for the cover design and to the printing services provided by Parry Global Solutions for our affordable, eco-friendly book.

Thank you to our partner funders and collaborators:

Pilot program funding for our "Earliest Teachable Moment" project, which led to our first cartoon-illustrated materials, is thanks to the Lucile Packard Foundation for Children's Health.

Funding to further develop and make available our cartoon materials for children is thanks to: Air Systems Foundation, Atkinson Foundation, Bank of the West, Bay Federal Credit Union, Best Buy @15C Community Grants Program, Brickyard Family Fund, Build-a-Bear Workshop Foundation, Cisco Systems Foundation, C.M. Capital Foundation, Colorado Trust, Community Health Foundation of Greater Petaluma, Community Foundation of Santa Cruz County, CVS/CareMark Charitable Trust, CVS/CareMark Community Grant, David and Lucile Packard Foundation, The Dean and Margaret Lesher Foundation, Driscoll's Charitable Fund, Ecolab, Embrey Family Foundation, Finish Line Youth Foundation, The June and Julian Foss Foundation, Frieda Fox Foundation, Freedom Rotary, Fremont Bank, Giant Steps Foundation, Google, The Health Trust, Hitachi America, Ltd., Hitachi Data Systems, Hitachi High Technologies America, Inc., Hitachi Foundation, Insurance Industry Charitable Foundation, In-N-Out Burger, Kaiser Permanente, Jean and Ed Kelly Foundation, Lowell Berry Foundation, CTB/McGraw-Hill, Mechanics Bank, Monterey Peninsula Foundation, Office Depot Foundation, Palo Alto Community Fund, Palo Alto Medical Foundation-Santa Cruz, Plantronics, Rite Aid Foundation, Robert and Aubrey Talbott Foundation, Safeway, San Francisco Foundation, Seagate, Smith Micro, Special Hope Foundation, Target Stores, TRIO Foundation, Verizon, Walmart, Wells Fargo Foundation, Western Digital, and Whole Foods.

Field-testing of our teaching materials is thanks to: Head Start of Santa Clara County, Head Start of San Mateo County, Marshall Pomeroy Elementary School of the Milpitas Unified School District, First Presbyterian Church of Burlingame Nursery School, the Special Education Department of the Santa Cruz County Office of Education, NHU/El Nuevo Mundo Bilingual Children's Center, and many other agencies and schools.

Copyright and Requirements for Permission to Use

Contact Information

Office	831-426-4407 or 1-800-467-6997 Ext. #1
Fax	831-426-4480
Email	safety@kidpower.org
Webpage	www.kidpower.org
Address	P.O. Box 1212, Santa Cruz, CA 95061, USA

kidpower™
Safety Comics
*For Younger Children **Ages 3 to 10** and Their Adults*

Table of Contents

Important Information for Adults

For Adults and Children to Read and Practice Together

Welcome to Kidpower!

Thank you for taking the time to learn and teach "People Safety" skills to the children in your life! We use the term "People Safety" to mean people being emotionallly and physically safe with people, including themselves and others. This comic book is targeted toward children from about ages three to ten who are usually with adult caregivers. These skills, ideas and teaching methods are also appropriate for younger and older children - indeed for adults too!

This book is divided into two sections. The first section, *Important Information for Adults*, is designed to help you prepare to teach and discuss People Safety skills with children. The second section, *For Adults and Children to Read and Practice Together*, is full of clearly illustrated examples and stories specifically designed for introducing these safety skills in the context of daily life.

When teaching safety skills to children, please keep these important ideas in mind:

Teaching children about People Safety works best if it is done in a way that is fun instead of scary. If adults discuss upsetting reasons why children might need to learn how to be safe with people, children are more likely to become anxious or resistant. Through calm conversations, fun hands-on practice, and enthusiastic encouragement, you can prepare children to keep themselves safe most of the time.

Children learn better by doing than by being told what to do. As much as you can, give children chances to PRACTICE every skill you teach them. You can have them act out what they see the children in the drawings doing to keep themselves safe, while you pretend to be the person in the drawings who is not following the safety rules. You can integrate People Safety skills into your daily life, coaching children so they are successful - in the same way that you might prepare children to be safe with water, food, fire, cars, and bikes.

Listen to children and show them that they are important to you. The best way to help children be safe is for them to have caring adults in their lives who they trust to go to when they have a problem. No matter how busy you are, ask children calmly, "Is there anything you have been worrying or wondering about?" Listen to their answers and thank them for telling you. No matter how many things they do wrong, tell children often, "I love you just the way you are."

Kidpower brings self-protection and confidence skills to children, teenagers, and adults, including those with special needs, across many different cultures around the world. Our services include workshops, long distance training and coaching, publications, and an extensive, free on-line Library. Visit www..kidpower.org.

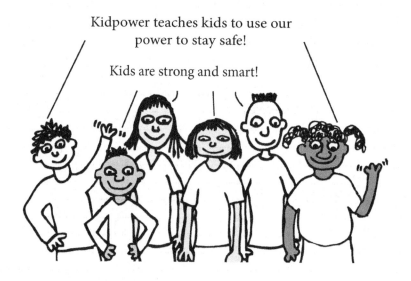

Kidpower teaches kids to use our power to stay safe!

Kids are strong and smart!

How to Use This Book

1 Read the book yourself. Notice how many of these ideas and skills are important for adults too.

2 Read the relevant sections of the book with your children. Point out the different ways that children in the stories are solving a variety of People Safety problems.

3 Practice the skills shown in the drawings. Each skill set is explained on pages 6-7.

I'll pretend to be somebody you don't know. We'll take turns having each of you practice moving away and checking first.

4 Encourage children to use their skills out in the world and throughout the day.

Thank you for checking first. Let's ask the person this dog is helping.

May I pet the dog?

Some Ways You Can Help Children Be Safe

1 Stay calm. Children learn better when their grownups are calm.

Stay with me when we cross the street.

2 Supervise children closely. They are too young to be on their own. Their safety is more important than anything else.

Sorry! You have to wait until I can go with you.

3 Make a safety plan for how to get help everywhere you go. The Safety Plan will be different for different people, at different times of the day, and in different places.

BIG STORE

Stay with me, but if you get lost, remember your Safety Plan and go to the checkout counter.

4 Give children chances to practice their People Safety skills everywhere you go.

What do you do if someone knocks on the door?

Find you and Check First!

Knock Knock

More Ways You Can Help Children Be Safe

5 Help children be successful in practicing skills by coaching them to handle problems in the moment.

You can say, "Please stop! I am using that toy. Wait until I'm done."

6 Help children understand about strangers. Tell them most people are good, but if they do not know someone well, their Safety Plan is to check with you right away.

Most strangers are good. But come check with me first!

7 Set a good example. Solve problems peacefully, respectfully, and powerfully. Children will learn more by what they see you doing than by what you tell them to do.

Hey! You took my parking space, you @&%$!

Sorry! It was an accident! I didn't see you.

8 Listen to children. Respect their feelings, even if their worries seem silly to you.

Thank you for telling me. We can leave your door open, or put a nightlight on, or give you a flashlight!

The dark makes me scared...

Kidpower's Underlying Principle

The safety and self-esteem of a child are more important than anyone's embarrassment, inconvenience or offense.

Discussions and Practices
To Build Understanding and Skills

The *Kidpower Safety Comics* provides tools for adults to use in introducing "People Safety" ideas and skills to children who are usually with adults who can help them. We recommend that you read the stories together, act out what the people are doing in the drawings, and discuss how these ideas might work in your daily lives. Practice skills with children for short periods of time and review the skills often to show how they can be helpful in a variety of different situations. Give special attention to actions that might be hard due to embarrassment, such as interrupting busy adults when you have a safety problem, yelling to get help, or speaking up if someone is bullying. Let children know that feeling embarrassed, upset, or shy is normal, but it is important not to let these emotions stop them from getting help or making the safest choices.

Adapt your approach and examples to be relevant for each child's age, life situation, and abilities. If necessary, simplify the information by using fewer words or change the wording to ensure understanding. You can also expand on the concepts presented by working with your child to figure out how to use these skills and ideas to handle more complicated situations that might not be covered in this book.

With each activity, remember to tell younger children that "I am just pretending so that we can practice!" This reminder helps prevent more literal children from having hurt feelings or becoming confused when you pretend to be a stranger or someone who is speaking or acting in an unkind way.

Instead of testing or tricking children, coach them to be successful. When you are practicing, pause to give them a chance to do the skill. If they get stuck, coach them in exactly what to say, how to say it, and what to do with their bodies, as if you were the director in a play. Make the practices fun by being positive and calm rather than anxious. Reward small steps with encouragement, remembering that mistakes are part of learning. Celebrate progress rather than looking for perfection.

Here are some ways to practice specific skills with children:

Be aware, calm and confident (Page 12)
Explain that, "People bother you less and listen to you more if you are aware, calm and confident." Have children stand or sit tall and turn their heads to look around. Walk behind them and do something silly for them to look at. Ask them to tell you what they saw so you know they are really looking around.

Use different kinds of power and move out of reach (Pages 13, 14, and 15)
We want children to know that there are many ways to be powerful. Coach children to squeeze their lips together to use Mouth Closed Power. Coach children to raise their hands *as if* to hit or touch something they shouldn't and instead pull their hands down to their sides to use Hands Down Power. Coach children to put their hands in front of themselves like a fence and say, "Stop!" to use Stop Power. Pretend to be another kid who is starting to get mad, or who is about to throw things or shove on the playground or in line. Coach children to use their Walk Away Power to move out of reach. With your child, you can come up with even more ideas of different ways to be powerful.

Use the coaching guides on the bottom of page 11 to practice Moving Out Of Reach. Start close together and have your child practice backing away. You can then act out the Leaving Story and the Line Story by pretending to be a grumpy kid and having your child practice moving away from you with awareness, calm and confidence.

Check First to be safe (Pages 16, 17, 18 and 19)
Unless children are independent enough to be somewhere or do something without an adult supervising their safety, their first line of self-protection is to Check First with their adults before they change their plan about what they are doing, whom they are with, or where they are going. Practice the Check First rule using relevant examples from a child's life such as: before you open the door, before you use the stove, before you get close to an animal at the park (you can use a toy animal to pretend), before you pick up something sharp, and before you get close to someone you don't know well. Coach the child to stand up, move away, and go to her or his adult to Check First.

Know how to be safe with strangers (Pages 20, 21 and 22)

During your daily life, point out people who are strangers and people who children know well. Pretend to be a stranger. Approach the child calling the child's name or holding something that belongs to the child. Coach the child to stand up, move away and go to his or her adult to Check First. You can have another adult or child or even a toy pretending to be this child's grownup. Have this person say, "Thank you for checking first!" While you are pretending to be the "stranger," act like someone who just doesn't know the safety rules rather than being scary. Help your child to be successful and to reinforce keeping a distance from people the child doesn't know by never getting too close to him or her (always maintain a distance of at least 6 feet away from your child when you are practicing Stranger Safety skills).

Know your Safety Plan if you are having an emergency or are lost (Pages 23 and 24)

Children need to know the exceptions to the Check First rules. Make and review your family's Safety Plan for getting help each time your child goes to a new place. Encourage children to buy something from the cashier so that they know how to interact with this person. Take children to the place you want them to go if they are lost or bothered in a store or out in public. Make sure they can find this place if they need help. If children cannot follow their Safety Plan, discuss back-up plans for getting help that make sense for that situation, such as asking a woman with children, calling police, etc. Unless they are having a big emergency, children should not leave the place you were planning for them to be. Be clear that the rules are different in emergencies.

We want children to get help when they are hurt or in trouble if they cannot immediately get help from their adults. Getting help in public can be embarrassing. Pretend to be a busy, impatient cashier and coach children to come to the front of the line, interrupt you, and be persistent in asking for help because they are being bothered by someone, their friend is hurt, or they are lost. Practice with children yelling for help as if they hurt their leg and can't move or as if they are lost in the woods.

Yell, leave and get help if you are scared (Page 26)

Pretend to be someone acting a little unsafe (not in a frightening way). Say something like "Hey kid, get over here!" but do not say something that might put a scary or upsetting image in a child's head. Do not pretend to grab the child. Remember success-based learning -- coach your child to set a firm boundary and to use a strong yelling voice. Coach children to put their hands in front of themselves with their arms bent and palms facing out to make a wall and yell, "STOP!" As the pretend Scary Person, act startled and stop. Coach children to run, yelling "I NEED HELP! to their adults. Have the adult say, "I will help you."

Big kid being scary, showing arm grab escape (Page 27)

Practice the arm grab escape by grabbing a child's arm, and then coach her to grab that same arm with her other hand and pull away. The first time you practice, let go when you feel the child pull against you. Then let the child practice again and hold on a little tighter. Have the child pull her hands out against the place where your fingertips come together with your thumb, because this spot is the weakest part of someone's grip. Have the child yell, "NO!" and "HELP!" loudly while pulling away.

The rule is that touch and games for fun or affection have to be okay with each person, safe, allowed by the adults in charge, and NOT a secret (Pages 33, 34 and 35)

Play the "Asking for a hug"" game by having children ask you, "May I have a hug?" Say, "No thanks. No hugs today. We can wave." And wave. Then reverse roles and ask, "May I have a hug?" Coach children to say, "No thanks. No hugs today. Just wave." And wave. This practice lets children practice setting and accepting boundaries on unwanted touch for affection.

Protect your feelings from hurting words (Page 30 and 31)

Children are emotionally safest if they can take in the nice things people say to them or they say to themselves and protect themselves from the hurting words. Have children pretend to catch hurting words in the air, throw them into a real trash can or a trash can they make with their bodies and say something nice to themselves. Put a hand on your hip and show that the hole makes a personal Trash Can. Practice together - for example, if someone says, "You' are stupid," children can catch the word "STUPID," throw it in their personal Trash Can and say, "I am SMART!" Make sure children know that you are just pretending so they can practice and that you do not mean the words you are saying. Do not have children practice saying hurtful words -- you want them to focus on the skill of protecting their feelings.

Give children meaningful compliments for them to take in.to their hearts while saying, "Thank you!" Have them practice giving compliments to each other -- and to you!

Stop unwanted touch or teasing (Page 37)

These skills prepare children to persist in setting boundaries if someone doesn't notice, doesn't listen, tries to make them wrong, offers a bribe, or makes them promise not to tell. Teach children to use their voices, bodies, and words to set clear boundaries with people they know, such as family, friends, and peers.

1. Touch children on the shoulder and ask them if they like it. If they like it, that is fine, but they can also change their minds. Have them pretend they don't like it anymore and coach children to give you back your hand and say, in a clear, firm voice, "Please stop."

2. Pretend not to listen; put your hand back. Coach children to stand or move back, make a fence with their hands, look at you and say in a calm, firm voice, and say, "I said, 'Please stop!' I don't like it."

3. Next, pretend to be sad or annoyed so children can practice dealing with emotional coercion. Say, "But I like you. I thought you were my friend." Coach children to project an assertive attitude while they say, "I don't mean to hurt your feelings and I am your friend, and I still want you to stop." Or just, "Sorry and stop!"

4. Discuss when bribes are safe or unsafe. Practice resisting unsafe bribes. Say, "I'll give you a treat (offer something you think the child you are working with would like) if you let me touch your shoulder after you asked me to stop. But don't tell anybody, okay?" Coach each child to say, "Stop or I'll tell!" You can have them add, "I don't keep touch or gifts a secret."

5. For children who can understand (normally children over 5 or 6 years old) give them the chance to practice promising not to tell even though they are going to tell an adult they trust as soon as they can. Pretend to get angry or upset (but please don't act too intensely) and say, "Promise not to tell anyone or something bad will happen!" Coach children to say, "I won't tell if you stop." Be clear that they can lie and break a promise to keep themselves safe. If this happens, their safety plan is to tell an adult they trust as soon as they can, and to keep telling until they get help.

Go and get help when you have a problem and keep trying until you get help (Pages 36 and 39)

Remind children that touch, games, presents, money, and problems should not be secrets. Discuss different safety problems children might have and who to ask for help if they need it. Tell children to pretend to have a safety problem. Pretend to be a busy adult (act as if you are reading a book, watching TV, or working). Coach children to interrupt you to ask for help. Say, "I'm busy." Coach children to ask again. Say, "Don't bother me." Coach children to say, "This is about my safety." Listen, coaching children to tell the whole story. Say, "Thank you for telling me." If children do this well, do the practice again but be unsupportive by saying, "That's your problem. Go away." Coach children to find another adult to tell.

Safety rules about private areas (Page 38)

It is very important to discuss your family's rules about private areas with your child in a calm and matter-a-fact way. Make sure to review this page with your child and review your safety rules about private areas about every six months.

Know what bullying is and how to stop it (Pages 40 and 41)

Point out examples of bullying as they happen in real life, in stories, or in movies such as shunning, name-calling, intimidation, etc. Pretend to act like a bully by saying something mean. Coach the child to use her or his Trash Can and move away. Or coach the child to say, "Stop," leave, and get help.

Do a practice where a child says, "I want to play." Or, "I want to join you." Pretend to reject the child by frowning and saying, "Go away. You're not good enough." Or, "There's too many already." Have the child throw away the hurting words and say, "I'm great." Coach the child to practice persisting instead of getting upset by saying, "I'll do my best." Or, "I'll get better if I practice." Or, "There's always room for one more." Or, "Give me a chance." Or, "The rule at school is everybody gets to play." Coach a child who is being left out to go find another child and invite that child to play.

Give a more verbal child the chance to practice being an advocate. Pretend to be unkind to someone else. Coach the child to say, "Stop. That is not kind!" Pretend to exclude another person so that the child can practice speaking up for someone else by saying, "Let her play!"

Pretend to be another child who is acting unsafely. Push the child gently and say something like, "Get over here, you dummy!" Coach the child to take a breath, throw the mean word away, use Mouth Closed Power by not answering back, and Walk Away Power by standing tall and leaving with awareness. Remind the child to go to an adult and get help because problems should not be secrets.

Be Aware, Calm, and Confident

People will bother you less and listen to you more when you are looking around, acting calm and confident, and staying in control of your body.

1 The boy is not paying attention and looks scared. This is **less safe.**

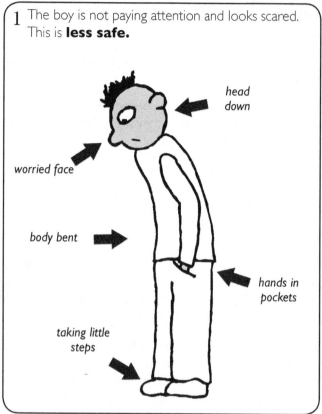

head down

worried face

body bent

hands in pockets

taking little steps

2 The boy looks aware and strong. This is **more safe.**

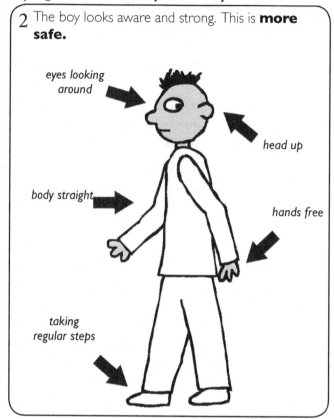

eyes looking around

head up

body straight

hands free

taking regular steps

3 The girl is acting mad. She looks like she wants to fight. This is **less safe.**

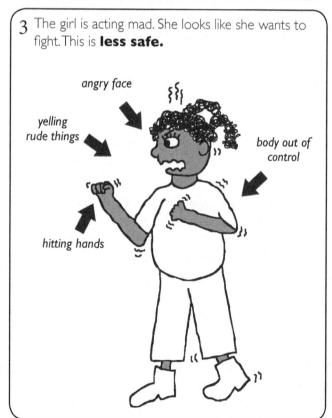

angry face

yelling rude things

body out of control

hitting hands

4 The girl looks calm and confident. This is **more safe.**

calm aware face

thinking, not yelling

body in control

hands down

Different Kinds of Power

1 The girl is rude and sticks out her tongue. The boy keeps his tongue and words in his mouth by using his **Mouth Closed Power** to stay safe.

((Rude noise))

2 The little boy hits his big brother. The big brother stops the hit and uses his **Hands Down Power** to keep himself from hitting back.

%&@%6@!!!!

Stop! No hitting!
Remember your
Hands Down Power.

3 The girl tries to grab the scooter. The boy uses his **STOP! Power** by having a strong voice and making a fence with his hands so he sounds and looks like he means it.

MY TURN!

WAIT! NO GRABBING!
You can use it when I'm
done.

4 The boy yells at his friend. The girl does *not* yell back. She uses her **Walk Away Power** to get away from his words and to stay safe.

I don't like you! I
don't like you!

The Leaving Story
Moving Out Of Reach

1 I like to dig with my friend in the sandbox.

2 When my friend gets mad and throws things, she can be mean to me too.

3 When my friend is in a bad mood, I can walk away.

4 I can play with other children or I can play by myself.

5 To practice moving out of reach, have the child start close and back up. Coach child to look at you and to glance back while backing up to make sure there is nothing to trip over.

6 Check to see if child is out of reach or needs to back up more. *Remember to coach child to be successful. Do not grab him if he is too close, just coach him to move back more.*

The Line Story

Moving Out Of Reach

1 Someone is pushing in line. I have not done or said anything, but the kid is still bothering me.

2 I wish she would stop pushing. But she does not notice and pushes more.

3 I get mad and push back. The teacher gets mad at both of us.

4 Next time that kid pushes, I leave the line and find another place. It is not important to be in front of the line. It is more important to be next to a kid who does not push.

Together or On Your Own

The rules are different if you are together with an adult who can help you or if you are on your own.

1 When you are right next to your mom at the store, you are together.

Together

2 Suppose the storekeeper has free samples. If your mom gives permission, you can take food from him.

Have some yummy free samples.

Yes, and thank you for checking first.

Mom, can I have some?

Together

3 If you and your mom are away from each other even a little bit, you are on your own. If your mom is in the next aisle and a lady has free samples...

Freshly made chocolate! Free samples!

Oooh, I love chocolate... But I am on my own and need to Check First.

On Your Own

4 Your Safety Plan is to move away and go to your mom so you can Check First.

Freshly made chocolate! Free samples!

Thank you for checking first. Let's get some together.

Mom, can I have some chocolate?

Move Away and Check First

Where is Safety...?

Safety is where you can find safe adults to help you.

1 ...at my **school**?

My teacher is safety!

2 ...at my **home**?

My grownups are safety!

3 ...at **my home when my adults are not there**?

My child care person is safety!

4 ...at **my friend's house**?

My friend's grandma is safety!

5 ...at **the store**?

The checkout person is safety!

6 ...at **the amusement park**?

The ticket person is safety!

TICKETS

Checking First to Be Safe

1 **Check First** with your adults before you play with animals unless you know them very well.

2 **Check First** with your adults before you get out of your car seat, unhook your seat belt, or go out of the car.

3 **Check First** with your adults before you go out the gate, out the door, or out of the house, even if something very interesting is happening.

4 **Check First** with your adults before you touch the stove, plug anything into an electric outlet, or play with matches.

The Pizza Story

Check First Before You Change Your Plan

1 The boy and his sister are walking home after school.

2 Their dad drives up. He asks if they want pizza.

Let's get pizza!

Yeah, pizza!

3 Their mom is working at home. When her children don't come home after school, she gets worried. She tries to figure out where they are.

4 When their mom can't find her kids, she calls the police. They find the kids and their dad at the pizza parlor.

Hello, police. I am so worried. My kids aren't home and I don't know where they are.

5 Mom is very glad and very mad.

WHY DIDN'T YOU CALL ME?!

We forgot. From now on, we will CHECK BEFORE WE CHANGE THE PLAN!

6 A few days later, their next door neighbor invites the kids to come over. They've been at his house before, but they remember to **check before they change their plans**.

Come on over. I just baked cookies.

We'd love to visit, but we need to CHECK FIRST!

What's a Stranger?

A stranger is just someone you don't know well. Strangers can look like anybody.

1

A stranger is just a person you do not know well. Most strangers are good. But check with me before you talk or get close to strangers.

Are strangers bad?

2

Teacher, are you a stranger? Are these other kids strangers?

Today is the first day of school so we are strangers to each other. When we get to know each other, we will not be strangers. It's okay to be here because your parents said it was okay.

3

People wearing uniforms are also strangers. Police officers. Fire fighters. Check with me first.

Is that police officer a stranger?

4

When does someone stop being a stranger and start being somebody we know?

Good question. A person stops being a stranger after we know that person really well. Ask me if you are not sure.

Checking First Rules With Strangers

If you are on your own, go to your adult and Check First before you **take** anything from, **get close** to, or **talk** to a stranger.

1 Before you take anything from a stranger, even if it is yours...

2 Check First!

3 Before you open the door...

4 Check First!

5 Before you get close to or talk with a stranger...

6 Check First!

More Times to Check First

1 If someone else has an emergency.

My child is lost. Please look!

This is a stranger. I will get help by CHECKING FIRST.

2 If someone is wearing a uniform.

A kid is hurt. Come with me to help!

This is a stranger. I am going to CHECK FIRST and get my grownups to help!

The Stranger Knows My Name Story

1 I am playing in the hall by my apartment. A stranger calls my name.

Hi Hideko!

Who is that?!

2 She is nice, but I move away.

Don't you remember me? I am a friend of your mom!

I Check First.

A stranger knows my name!

Thank you for telling me!

My grownup helps me.

Hideko did not remember me!

That is ok! I am proud that she remembered her safety rules!

Getting Help in Emergencies

If you have an **emergency** and cannot **Check First**, your
Safety Plan is to **get help** even from someone you don't know.

1 You can get help from paramedics.

2 You can get help from firefighters.

3 You can get help from a search party.

4 You can get help from a woman with children in an EMERGENCY.

Your Safety Plan if You Are Lost in a Store

1 Everywhere you go, make a safety plan with your grownup for what to do if you get lost.

Grandpa, what is our safety plan if we get lost?

Good question. Let's meet at checkout counter number one over there.

2 The first thing to do if you are lost is stand tall and still like the trunk of a tree and look around to see if you can find your grownup.

Where's Grandpa?

3 The next thing to do is yell for your grownup.

GRANDPA!

4 If that does not work, go to the front of the checkout line, not the back. Interrupt the cashier and ask for help.

I need help!

Go to the end of the line!

5 If the cashier does not understand, ask again and say that you are lost.

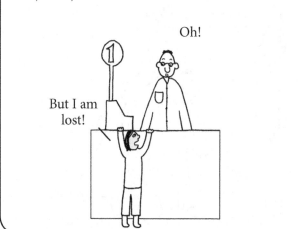

Oh!

But I am lost!

6 To help your grownup find you, you may need to tell the cashier your grownup's name.

We have a lost girl here...

There you are!

When to Wait and When to Interrupt

You might have to **wait** if you **want** something.
Interrupt and keep asking for help if there is a **safety problem**.

1 You **wait** when your mom is busy on the computer even if you want to talk to her.

2 You **interrupt** your mom when the pot is boiling over on the stove.

3 You **wait** when your Dad is on the phone even if he has been talking forever.

4 You **interrupt** your dad when a kid is hurting another kid.

5 You go to the end of the line and **wait** your turn when you want to buy something in a store.

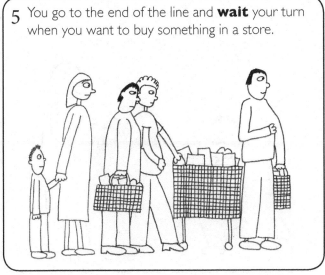

6 You go to the front of the line and **interrupt** the cashier so you can get help if you are lost in the store.

Yell, Leave, and Get Help if You Are Scared

1 A big kid pushes me. I am scared.

2 I yell, run, and go to my teacher for help.

3 A dog is acting mean. I am scared.

4 I tell the dog firmly to stop. I back away and go to my mom for help.

5 Some kids are very angry. I am scared.

6 I yell, run, and go to the yard duty person for help.

The Big Kid Being Scary Story

Yelling in a strong voice and running to an adult to get help can help keep you safe.

1 I like to go to the store with my mom.

2 A big kid grabs me and I am scared.

3 I pull my arm away and yell.

NO!!

4 I use my Stop Sign and a big voice to scare the big kid.

NO!

5 I run and yell for help.

I NEED HELP!!

6 My mom helps me and the big kid is sorry.

It's not funny to scare little kids.

I'm sorry.

Introduction to Boundaries

A boundary is like a fence. It sets a limit. Personal boundaries are the limits between people. We have to set boundaries with ourselves and with each other.

The rules about personal boundaries are:

We each belong to ourselves. You belong to you and I belong to me. This means that your body belongs to you— AND so does your personal space, your feelings, your time, your thoughts— ALL of you! This means that other people belong to themselves too.

Some things are not a choice. This is true for adults as well as kids. Especially for kids, touch for health and safety is often not a choice.

Problems should not be secrets. Anything that bothers you, me, or anybody else should not have to be a secret, even if telling makes someone upset or embarrassed. Also, presents, games, or any kind of touch should not have to be a secret..

Keep telling until you get help. When you have a problem, find an adult you trust and keep on telling until you get the help you need.

1 We each belong to ourselves.

Hehe... weeee!

2 Some things are not a choice.

You need a bath!

NO BATH!

Problems should not be secrets.

Keep telling until you get help.

But Grandpa I'm very sad!

Zzz... sad?!

The Bath Story

This story shows how the boundary rules can work in real life.

1 We each belong to ourselves.

Bath Time!

My body belongs to me and I don't have to take a bath!

2 Some things are not a choice.

Your body does belong to you, but you still have to take a bath!

3 Problems should not be secrets.

I will tell!

Great! Tell the WHOLE world that your mother made you take a bath!

4 Keep telling until you get help.

The mom in this story did the right thing by saying the little girl could tell if she wanted to.

The safety rule is that kids should be able to talk with adults they trust about anything that bothers them.

But, suppose that this girl's mom had said, "Please don't tell! That would be too embarrassing."

If the mom had done this, she would have been making a safety mistake. Even though taking a bath was not the girl's choice, she should be able to talk about her feelings.

The Trash Can for Hurting Words

**If people say hurting words to you, you can protect your feelings.
Throw the hurting words away and tell yourself something good.**

1 You can imagine catching hurting words instead of taking them into your heart.

2 Throw the hurting words into the trash while you say something nice to yourself.

3 Put your hand on your hip. Imagine the hole it makes is your Kidpower Trash Can. Catch hurting words, push them through your Trash Can, and say something good to yourself.

4 You can use your Trash Can anytime.

5 You can make your Trash Can with your mind.

6 You can use your Trash Can when you say hurting things to yourself.

Taking in Compliments

Compliments are nice words. They help you feel good about yourself. When someone gives you a compliment, you can take it inside your heart and say, "Thank you!"

1 The boy tells his older brother that he looks cool. His big brother throws the compliment away.

2 The little brother tries again because he wants his big brother to take good words into his heart, not throw them away.

3 The girl likes what her little sister built. The little sister throws the compliment away.

4 The big sister tells her again. She wants her little sister to believe the compliment.

Choice and Not a Choice

Your body belongs to you, but some things are not a choice.

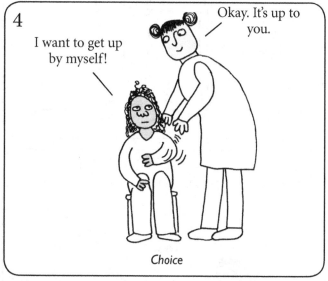

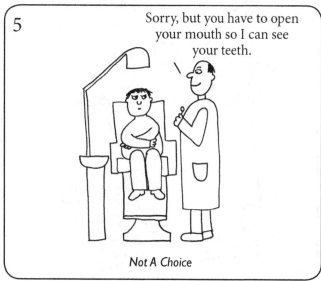

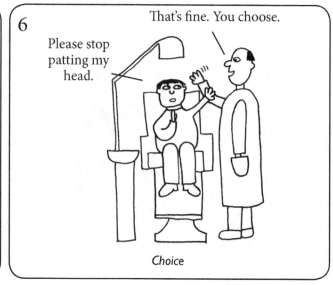

Safety Rules on Touch and Play for Fun and for Affection

Should be the choice of each person, safe, okay with the adults in charge, and not secret.

1

Choice of Both People

2

Tickle tickle!

Stop that game. I don't like it!

Not the Choice of Both People

3

Safe

4

Be careful! That is NOT safe!

Not Safe

5

Thank you for wiping her face.

Okay with the Grownups in Charge

6

NO playing with FOOD! That is NOT allowed!

Not Okay with the Grownups in Charge

The Sloppy Kisses Story

1 I like to give my big sister sloppy kisses

2 Sometimes she does not like it. This means I have to stop even if I still want to give her kisses.

3 My sister can love me and I can love her and she can still tell me to stop.

4 Kisses have to be okay with both people.

5 Now we are both happy.

6 When my aunt comes to visit, I can tell her what kinds of kiss I want. Kisses have to be the choice of both people.

Safety with Touch Means You Can Always Tell

1 Touch for health and safety is not a choice.

2 Problems with touch or anything else should not be secrets.

3 If something bothers you, you can tell all your grownups.

4 If you like kissing your grandpa, that's nice.

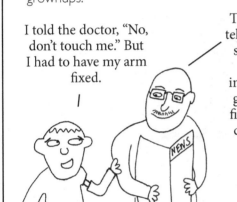

5 It is always okay to change your mind.

6 You can always tell what happened.

The Overnight Story

Anytime you have a problem, even if you need to wake up a grownup
in the middle of the night, your job is to get help.

1 My cousin and I have fun when I stay overnight.

2 When the lights are out, we cuddle together to feel safe in the dark.

3 My cousin takes too much space, and I fall out of bed. I am not comfortable, and I can't sleep.

4 I go get help from my aunt even though it is the middle of the night.

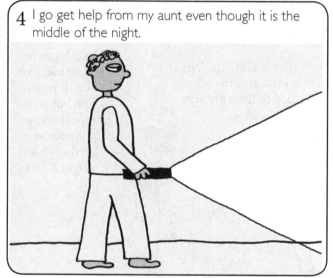

5 My aunt just wants me to go back to bed. I keep telling her until she understands and helps me.

6 My aunt makes a bed for me on the couch so I can be comfortable.

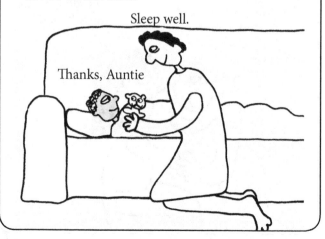

How to Stop Unwanted Touch

Your body belongs to you. You can tell people to stop if you do not like touch or games like kisses, hugs, roughhousing, tickling, or jokes.

1 If you like it when your friend tickles you, it is fine.

2 You can change your mind. Use your eyes, words, and body to tell your friend when you want him to stop.

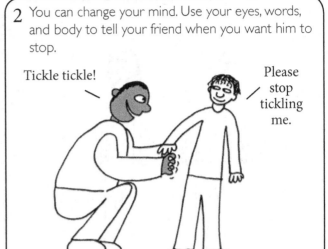

3 If he does not listen, you can stand up, move away, make a fence with your hands, and say stop.

4 If your friend is sad or mad because you told him to stop, tell him that you are sorry but he still has to stop.

5 Gifts or favors should not break the safety rules about touch or games, and should not be a secret.

6 Even if you have to promise not to tell, the safety rule is to go **tell** and keeping telling until you get help.

Safety Rules About Touching Private Areas

1 Private areas are the parts of your body that can be covered by a bathing suit.

2 For play or teasing, other people should not touch your private areas. They should not ask you to touch their private areas either.

Let's take off our clothes so we can play doctor!

That is against our safety rules. We can play doctor with our clothes on.

3 Sometimes grownups have to touch kids' private areas to help them.

I need to put medicine on your sore.

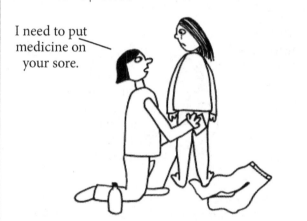

4 Touch of any kind should **never** be a secret.

Mom put medicine on my bottom today! I did not like it.

Thank you for telling me. I am sorry you didn't like it.

5 The safety rule is that people are not supposed to show you movies or pictures of people touching their private areas or without their clothes on.

Look at these pictures of grownups.

They don't have clothes on. Stop or I'll tell.

6 Even if the person stops, you should tell about anything that bothers you.

Thank you for telling me. We will help your cousin understand about the safety rules.

My cousin tried to show me pictures on his computer of people touching their private areas. I said, "Stop or I will tell."

The Keep Telling Until You Get Help Story

1 Today kids at school locked me in the bathroom. I was scared.

2 I tell my dog. He listens but he cannot help me.

Kids locked me in the bathroom. I was scared.

3 I tell my mom. She is too busy to understand.

Kids locked me in the bathroom. I was scared.

It's okay. Kids tease sometimes.

4 I tell my grandpa. He listens but not for very long.

Kids locked me in the bathroom. I was scared.

That's not nice. I had a hard day too. My boss got mad at me!

5 My safety rule is to tell a grownup I trust when I have problems and to keep telling until someone helps.

I will keep telling until someone helps me... who else can I talk to next?

6 My teacher listens. She understands and helps me.

Kids locked me in the bathroom at school yesterday. I was scared.

$1+1 = 2$
$2+2 = 4$
$4+4 = 8$

Oh my! Thank you for telling me. We will make sure you feel safe at school.

People Safety Skills to Stop Bullying

1 If somone tries to bully you by being scary, you can use your Walk Away Power and get help. Being mean back will make the problem bigger, not better.

Hey kid, I'm going to get you!

No thanks!

2 If someone tries to bully you by saying rude things, you can throw the hurting words in your Trash Can and say something kind to yourself.

Yuck! Your food looks weird!

My mom made my food and I like it!

YUCK

3 If someone tries to bully you by taking your turn, you can say, "NO!"

You HAVE to let me go first!

NO! Let go of my arm! It is my turn.

4 If someone tries to bully you by tripping or pushing, you can use your awareness to notice what this person is trying to do and then Move Out of Reach.

More Ways to Stop Bullying

5 If a friend tries to bully you by not letting you play with other people, you do not have to do what she or he says.

If you play with her, I won't be your friend anymore.

NO! True friends don't try to stop you from playing with other people.

6 If someone tries to bully you by not letting you join the game, you can keep asking. If you see this happen to someone else, you can speak up or get help.

No, we don't want you. You always drop the ball.

I will get better if I practice.

Let him play. The rule at school is everybody gets to play.

7 If some kids try to bully you by leaving you out, you can protect your feelings and find someone else to be your friend!

psst psst

Go away!

I will find another friend.

Go away!

8 You have the right to be safe with your feelings and your body. If you need help to stop bullying problems, you can ask the adults in charge.

Excuse me, I need help. Two boys tried to hit me.

I will help you.

Safety with Cars

1 Not Safe

Running into the street is not safe because you might get hit by a car.

2 Safe

Your safety rule is to **stop, look, and wait** for your grownup.

1 Not Safe

Even if you are with a grownup, it is not safe to walk in front of a car until it has stopped all the way.

2 Safe

Your safety rule is to **look** and **wait** until the street is clear or until the cars are all stopped.

1 Not Safe

BE CAREFUL!!

When a car backs up in a driveway, the driver cannot see a kid on a bike. It is not safe to go or ride your bike behind a backing up car.

2 Safe

Wait until the car is done backing up before you cross the driveway.

1 Not Safe

It is not safe to walk away from your grownup when you get out of your car.

2 Safe

Your safety rule is to stay next to your grownup when you are outside your car.

The Big Sister Story

Dedicated to the big sisters and big brothers everywhere who use their power to help keep their younger brothers and sisters safe!

1 My little brother wants to go out the door. I hold the door closed.

2 My little brother tries to climb out the window. I grab him and yell for help.

3 My little brother tries to get out of his car seat while we are driving. I yell for help.

4 My little brother tries to climb over the wall and into the water with the ducks. I grab him and yell for help. My little brother is annoyed. My parents thank me for stopping him from falling into the pond, while still staying safe myself.

What is Kidpower?

Kidpower Teenpower Fullpower International™ (shortened to Kidpower™) is a charitable nonprofit organization founded in Santa Cruz, California in 1989. Our vision is to work together to create cultures of caring, respect, and safety for everyone. Our mission is to empower people of different ages and abilities by helping them learn how to stay safe, act wisely, and believe in themselves. Experts highly recommend the Kidpower approach for being positive, practical, hands-on, emotionally and physically safe, and relevant.

Kidpower teaches people of different ages and abilities to be successful in learning and practicing personal safety, self-protection, confidence, boundary-setting, and advocacy skills. These "People Safety" skills prepare individuals from all walks of life to prevent and stop most bullying, harassment, molestation, assault, abduction, and other kinds of violence and abuse — and to advocate effectively for the well-being of themselves and others. Since 1989, Kidpower has brought People Safety education to more than 2 million children, teenagers, and adults, including those with special needs, of many different cultures -- locally and around the world.

Our services are:

- developed to work well for the different life situations and ages of our students.
- designed to be upbeat, effective, safe, emotionally supportive, and hands-on.
- tailored to fit the specific needs of your family, circle of friends, school, organization, service club, or business.
- adapted for people who face special physical, emotional, or developmental challenges.

Our website at www.kidpower.org will give you access to our:

- Free e-newsletter with useful articles and safety tips, reviews of books and videos, how to bring People Safety skills to others, practices for building better relationships, etc.
- Free Library of articles on a wide range of People Safety topics, along with PDFs you can share.
- Free audio podcasts and videos.
- Safety Store with publications and other educational resources for sale.
- Service information about who we serve and what we do.

Where Are Kidpower Services Available?

Kidpower has centers and representatives in the United States, Canada, Mexico, Europe, Asia, Africa, South America, and Oceania. We adapt our services to meet the needs of different cultures.

Our skills have been taught successfully in Arabic, Cantonese, French, German, Greek, Hebrew, Italian, Spanish, Swedish, Urdu, Vietnamese, and other languages as well as English. In August, 2005, we conducted an international conference in Montreal to train professionals from charitable organizations serving young people who face difficult life challenges. Since then, through our Reaching Out project, professionals from nonprofit organizations in developing countries are learning how to use the Kidpower Method of teaching People Safety skills to help the vulnerable children, teens, and adults that they serve.

Please Join Us in Bringing Kidpower to Everyone, Everywhere!

Learn about People Safety skills and concepts for yourself and teach them to others. Join us on Facebook. Make a tax-deductible contribution through our website at **www.kidpower. org**. Recommend Kidpower to your company, family, or service club for charitable and volunteer support. Tell others about the resources Kidpower has to offer.

Thank you!

CPSIA information can be obtained at www.ICGtesting.com
Printed in the USA
LVOW04s1718291014

411095LV00015B/602/P

9 781479 147205